Helen Keller
and the
Big Storm

written by
Patricia Lakin

illustrated by
Diana Magnuson

Ready-to-Read

Aladdin

New York   London   Toronto   Sydney   Singapore

For Erika Tamar . . .
who always brings me back to my senses.
—P.L.

To Samantha.
Thanks for making it real.
—D.M.

First Aladdin edition January 2002

Text copyright © 2002 by Patricia Lakin

Illustrations copyright © 2002 by Diana Magnuson

Aladdin Paperbacks

An imprint of Simon & Schuster

Children's Publishing Division

1230 Avenue of the Americas

New York, NY 10020

CHILDHOOD OF FAMOUS AMERICANS is a registered trademark

of Simon & Schuster, Inc.

READY-TO-READ is a registered trademark of Simon & Schuster, Inc.

The text for this book was set in 17 Point Utopia

Designed by Lisa Vega

The illustrations were rendered in acrylic

Printed and bound in the United States of America

20 19

The Library of Congress has Cataloged the paperback edition as follows:

Lakin, Pat.

Helen Keller and the big storm / written by Patricia Lakin ; illustrated by Diana Magnuson.

p. cm.–(Childhood of famous Americans series)

Summary: A true incident in the life of young Helen Keller in which she gets stuck in a storm and her
teacher, Annie Sullivan, rescues her.

ISBN 978-0-689-84104-0 (pbk.)

0121 LAK

1. Keller, Helen, 1880-1968—Childhood and youth—Juvenile literature. 2. Blind-deaf women—United
States—Biography—Juvenile literature. 3. Sullivan, Annie, 1866-1936—Juvenile literature. [1. Keller,
Helen, 1880-1968—Childhood and youth. 2. Sullivan, Annie, 1866-1936. 3. Blind. 4. Deaf. 5. Physically
handicapped. 6. Women—Biography.] I. Magnuson, Diana, ill. II. Title. III. Series.

HV1624.K4 L34 2002

362.4'1'092—dc21

[B]

2001033818

Helen Keller
and the
Big Storm

Little Helen Keller loved
smelling roses and honeysuckle.
They grew all around
her Alabama home.

But most of all,
Helen loved playing pranks.
When she was six, she had done
her best prank yet!
Mamma had walked
into the
kitchen pantry.

Quickly, Helen felt for the key.
Click! Helen locked Mamma inside.
Helen didn't always have the chance
to take charge like that.
Mamma and Papa tried hard
to understand her.
But many times no one knew
what she wanted.

Helen could get so angry,
she would kick and hit
and fall into a heap.

Afterward, she ran outside.
She threw herself onto
the cool, comforting grass.
The flowers, trees, grass,
warm sun, and gentle wind
always made Helen feel better.

Helen was never punished
for her pranks and tantrums.
Mr. and Mrs. Keller thought
Helen had been punished enough.
Their daughter could not hear,
or see, or talk.
But that pantry prank
forever changed Helen's life.
The Kellers now knew
that Helen needed more
than they could give her.
She needed special lessons
from a special teacher.

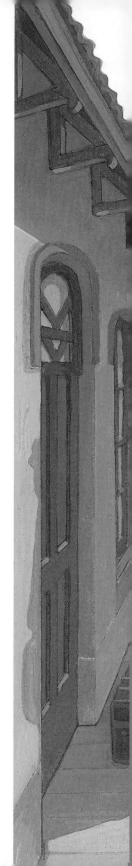

Helen's teacher was Annie Sullivan.

She came to live with the Kellers.

Helen was not ready

to trust this stranger.

And she was not ready

to give up her pranks.

She locked Annie inside her room.

And this time Helen hid the key!

That prank made Annie see

just how clever Helen was.

No matter what Helen did,

Annie did not give up!

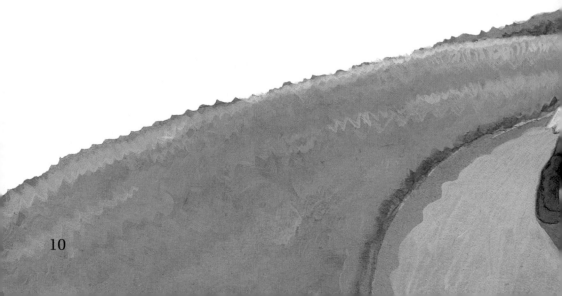

Slowly, day by day,
she worked with Helen.
Annie taught Helen
by pressing her fingers
into Helen's hand.
Annie's fingers spelled out the names
for the things Helen loved.
Grass. Flowers. Leaves. Trees. Bugs.
Butterflies. Sun. Wind. Rain.
In a short time, Helen loved
doing her lessons
more than doing her pranks.

Soon, the out-of-doors

became Helen's classroom.

One summer day,

Helen and Annie took a long walk.

On their way home,

the air grew hot and sticky.

Helen and Annie stopped to rest
under a wild cherry tree.
The tree blocked them
from the burning hot sun.
Its leaves fanned them
with a gentle, cooling breeze.

Helen felt its strong, low branches.

They were just right for climbing.

Annie and Helen decided to do just that!

Sitting high in the tree, they had
a resting-place to stay cool.
It was a perfect spot for a picnic!

Annie headed for the house
to make the lunch.
She made Helen promise
not to move an inch.
Helen wouldn't think of moving.
She loved sitting
high up in that tree!

Helen breathed in the wonderful scent
of the cherry tree.
She stroked its rough bark
and its smooth green leaves.
She let the cooling breeze blanket her.

But in seconds,
Helen's world
turned upside down.
The sun disappeared.
Helen's face was slapped
with a cold, sharp wind.

The scent of flowers was gone.
Her nose was filled
with another smell.
This one was not sweet.
It came up from
the deep, dark earth.
It told Helen that
a storm was near.
Helen began to feel
the shaking of the leaves.
Twigs rained down,
scratching her face,
arms, and legs.

Tree limbs swayed.
The wind whipped
through the branches.
The wind whipped
around Helen.
The wind tried to rip Helen
right out of that tree.

Helen grabbed onto
the shaking branch.
She clung to it
with all of her might.
Helen sat frozen.

She was trapped.

She could not see.

She could not call for help.

She could not hear

if help was on the way.

Helen had never felt

so alone or so scared.

She couldn't understand

how the gentle things she loved

could turn against her.

Suddenly, out of the
cold, whipping wind,
Helen felt a hand.
It was a strong, warm hand.
It belonged to Annie Sullivan.
Annie grabbed hold of Helen.
Helen let go of the branch.
She clung to Annie.
She let Annie guide her down
and out of that tree.

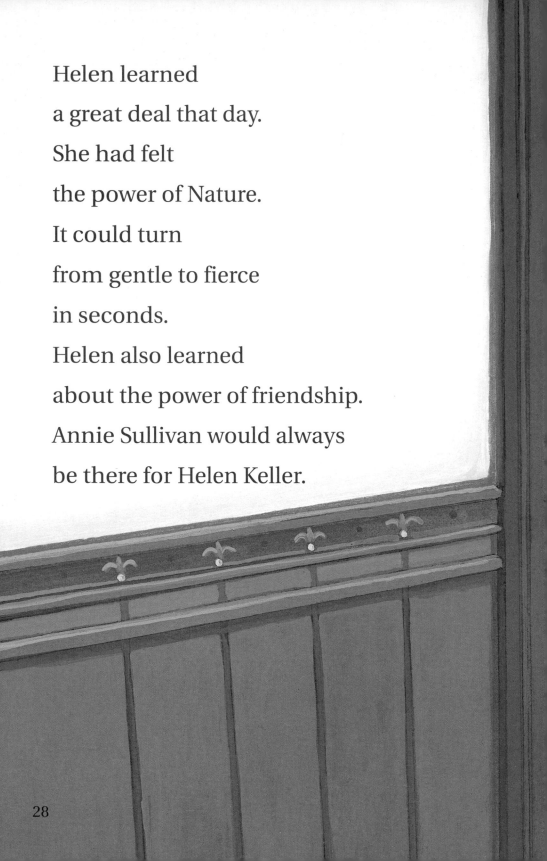

Helen learned
a great deal that day.
She had felt
the power of Nature.
It could turn
from gentle to fierce
in seconds.
Helen also learned
about the power of friendship.
Annie Sullivan would always
be there for Helen Keller.

Helen Keller and Annie Sullivan
were friends all of their lives.
Helen went on to become
a talented writer
who always worked
to help others.

Here is a timeline of Helen's life:

1880   Helen is born in Alabama.

1882   Illness leaves her deaf and blind.

1887   Teacher Annie Sullivan arrives at the Kellers'.

1888   With Annie, attends Boston's Perkins Institute for the Blind for a more formal education.

1900   Enters Radcliffe College—now part of Harvard University.

1902   Autobiography of Helen's early years is published.

1904   Graduates with honors from Radcliffe.

1923   Begins lifelong role as world-traveling spokesperson for the disabled.

1931   Named one of the twelve greatest living American Women.

1936   Annie Sullivan dies, and Mary Agnes (Polly) Thompson becomes Helen's companion.

1959   Broadway play *The Miracle Worker* opens. It is based on Annie and Helen's early years together. In 1962 it is made into a major motion picture.

1964   Receives the United States's highest civilian award, The Presidential Medal of Freedom.

1968   Dies at home in Connecticut.